When you invest your time, you make a goal and a decision of something that you want to accomplish. Whether it's make good grades in school, be a good athlete, be a good person, go down and do some community service and help somebody who's in need, whatever it is you choose to do, you're investing your time in that.

Nick Saban

I0420624

Don't walk through life just playing football. Don't walk through life just being an athlete. Athletics will fade. Character and integrity and really making an impact on someone's life, that's the ultimate vision, that's the ultimate goal - bottom line.

Ray Lewis

I wasn't a jock in school, and by the 10th grade, when I was in boarding school I was carrying water buckets for the girls' hockey team. I was the kid with long hair and glasses and acne trying to learn how to play guitar and piano in the music center. I was not an athlete past the age of 13 or 14 when they start throwing the ball really fast.

Michael Weatherly

We learn by practice. Whether it means to learn to dance by practicing dancing or to learn to live by practicing living, the principles are the same. One becomes in some area an athlete of God.

Martha Graham

The typical response from people when I tell them I'm diabetic is, 'Oh, I'm sorry to hear that.' You know, I'm not. I'm a better athlete because of diabetes rather than despite it. I'm more aware of my training, my fitness and more aware of nutrition. I'm more proactive about my health.

Charlie Kimball

Whatever luck I had, I made. I was never a natural athlete, but I paid my dues in sweat and concentration and took the time necessary to learn karate and become world champion.

Chuck Norris

I don't recommend steroids for everyone, and I don't recommend growth hormones for everyone. But for certain individuals, I truly believe, because I've experimented with it for so many years, that it can make an average athlete a super athlete. It can make a super athlete - incredible. Just legendary.

Jose Canseco

Obviously, you're known for what you do. But you still want to be known as a good person. You're a person a lot longer before and after you're a professional athlete.

Derek Jeter

A good athlete always mentally replays a competition over and over, even in victory, to see what might be done to improve the performance the next time.

Frank Shorter

When should a college athlete turn pro? Not until he has earned all he can in college as an amateur.

Will Rogers

As a multisport athlete, I was always fascinated with competition and how to win. At HBS and later at the Harvard Department of Economics, I was drawn to the field of competition and strategy because it tackles perhaps the most basic question in both business management and industrial economics: What determines corporate performance?

Michael Porter

As a professional athlete a lot is going to be said about you - but I just try to move forward and try to achieve my goals.

LeBron James

In college I never realized the opportunities available to a pro athlete. I've been given the chance to meet all kinds of people, to travel and expand my financial capabilities, to get ideas and learn about life, to create a world apart from basketball.

Michael Jordan

First of all, I really never imagined myself being a professional athlete.

Bo Jackson

I realized I love motivating and I love empowering and I love inspiring people. I did that as an athlete for 18 years, and I am able to do that as a motivational speaker now as well as doing work on television.

Dominique Dawes

As an athlete, I understood the value of my health insurance. I knew that in my profession, injuries were common and could happen at any time.

Magic Johnson

Overall, I think Michael Jordan is the greatest athlete in any particular sport. He dominated the game for the Chicago Bulls and brought the NBA to its greatest peak of popularity.

Will McDonough

As an athlete, I used my speed, agility and quickness to go out and play against the big guys.

Michael Chang

I don't think being an athlete is unfeminine. I think of it as a kind of grace.

Jackie Joyner-Kersee

An athlete cannot run with money in his pockets. He must run with hope in his heart and dreams in his head.

Emil Zatopek

Truthfully, this is how I approach my workout: I want to be the best athlete I can possibly be. If I can out-perform some of the better athletes then I'm happy. When I look at the NFL or the NBA, these guys look how I want to look - it's useable, functional muscle.

Channing Tatum

To me, breakfast is my most important meal. It's often the meal you play a game on. I make sure I have oatmeal, milk, and fruit. It's the fuel you use to hopefully do your best, so eating right is a big part of being a professional athlete. I wish I paid more attention to it earlier in my life.

Andrew Luck

I learned that the only way you are going to get anywhere in life is to work hard at it. Whether you're a musician, a writer, an athlete or a businessman, there is no getting around it. If you do, you'll win - if you don't, you won't.

Bruce Jenner

Life is about being a versatile athlete and training in all realms of life.

Ray Lewis

An athlete who tells you the training is always easy and always fun simply hasn't been there. Goals can be elusive which makes the difficult journey all the more rewarding.

Alberto Salazar

If you look at any superior athlete, you will find a strong parental influence. Parents introduce their children to a sport, and then they support them.

Ivan Lendl

One minute you're a developing athlete trying to get to the top, then the next minute you do well and win a medal somewhere, and then it's all foisted on you. You never know when it's going to happen. You don't think about the media side of things when you're a young athlete trying to do well.

Jessica Ennis

People who aren't perhaps that into sport are going to be following me and wanting to be part of the Olympics. That definitely does bring added pressure but as an athlete the Olympics are the ultimate competition.

Jessica Ennis

I don't know if anything can really prepare you for 'Survivor,' but since I grew up as an athlete, the physical aspect came to me more easily.

Ethan Zohn

I would like to cite an instance which proves the efficacy of clean living on the part of an athlete coupled with the inspiration received from a champion which go a long way to making a champion.

Major Taylor

I'm not an athlete, I'm a baseball player.

John Kruk

I'm signing on to be an athlete, and it's almost like Karl Marx's theory on capitalism. I am both the worker and the product. I'm choosing to be a part of this system, thus I'm choosing to be part of the conditions that are set in this system.

Lawrence Jackson

Think about what caused the injury and how it can be prevented next time; that way, you will become a smarter athlete and less likely to repeat the same mistakes.

Kevin R. Stone

It is very dangerous to have your self-worth riding on your results as an athlete.

Jim Courier

One piece of advice that I would give to any young athlete or performer is remember to thank your mom.

Meryl Davis

I'd love to have a lasting impact as far as growing the game. It would be cool to be remembered as a major champion. I'd like to be remembered as a great golfer but also a great person, as far as growing the game and charity work. The whole well-rounded athlete.

Rickie Fowler

I have some cool talents. I'm really flexible and can do all sorts of twisted yoga positions. And I'm a big athlete and especially love soccer.

Genevieve Padalecki

If you look at all the sports in China, the government is extremely involved and they are extremely proud of their athlete.

Patrick Chan

When you grow up in life and you're poor, and because you're an athlete or you got rich overnight in music, unless you have access to financial advice or for the transition or matriculation of that process, then of course, you're going to go broke.

Steve Stoute

If an athlete takes a shortcut - literally, for example, by running a street that shortens the marathon route by a quarter mile - he or she doesn't have an insurmountable advantage. But it's an unfair advantage, and in a field of equally matched athletes, it's more than enough to make a difference.

Don Kardong

I've been a pretty selfish mom and a very unselfish athlete for about three years now and it's time to put my family first. It's probably time to move on.

Melanie Roach

I came out of my professional athlete career with a 450 credit score, no money in the bank to show for it, but I had an Ivy League degree. So I put that Dartmouth degree to good use and got a job on Wall Street. I hated it but used the time to make connections and become financially literate.

Brian J. White

Throughout my journey in basketball, I always have someone to talk to in my father. I know how hard he had to work as an athlete.

Joakim Noah

Also, I'd like to play an athlete again, while I'm still physically fit, or a musician, like Nat King Cole, because I play the trumpet and sing. I'd like to incorporate that into a character.

Adewale Akinnuoye-Agbaje

As an athlete, I'd average four hours a day. It doesn't sound like a lot when some people say they're training for 10 hours, but theirs includes lunch, massage and breaks. My four hours was packed with work.

Michael Johnson

There's nothing masculine about being competitive. There's nothing masculine about trying to be the best at everything you do, nor is there anything wrong with it. I don't know why a female athlete has to defend her femininity just because she chooses to play sports.

Rebecca Lobo

As an athlete, confidence makes me more competitive and helps me perform better.

Marlen Esparza

Being at school, being who I am, being an athlete, it was hard to find people like me. There's not many athletes that can be at my level. That was kind of hard finding people who love something so much they want to keep on doing it.

Sally Pearson

I'm a sports fan. I'm not just an athlete who plays football.

Reggie Bush

I was the first athlete, from a training standpoint, with Adidas to have their own signature shoe.

Keyshawn Johnson

I went through so many things personally, emotionally and mentally during that time off that I know that I'm better for it now and I think I'm a better athlete because of that.

Libby Trickett

He is very upbeat but we hear that all the time from just about any athlete.

Pat Cash

I think the greatest all-around athlete ever was Jim Brown. He played lacrosse, basketball and ran track at Syracuse. He played professional football for the Browns.

Will McDonough

I'm tall and thin but not strong, so you're either an athlete or you're funny.

Keegan-Michael Key

There's definitely a whole double standard. I don't understand it. A guy can be sexy and good-looking, and it totally just enhances his credibility as an athlete.

Lolo Jones

I'm an athlete; I've got an ego when stunt doubles have to come in. Not an ego like that, but when it comes to physical stuff, if I didn't have to have a stunt double, I would always probably do it myself unless the producers were jumping in and stopping me.

Michael B. Jordan

People were actually approaching me on the street and thinking that I was an athlete. They couldn't quite place it, but a runner, or swimmer or something.

Kristanna Loken

The Olympic Games are always in the head of every sports athlete. We work for that. The Olympics are the most important race. They're each four years, and everybody wants to show their best performance.

Tina Maze

When you reach that elite level, 90 percent is mental and 10 percent is physical. You are competing against yourself. Not against the other athlete.

Dick Fosbury

I am very optimistic, and I wish that God almighty grants me success to get a qualifying time. Only then can I go to the

Olympics. If this happens I will be the first Palestinian athlete to gain a qualifying time. This will be a big achievement.

Nader al-Masri

The holidays are important, but the path I've chosen doesn't take that into consideration. I do what I can to enjoy them, but it's one of the sacrifices of being an athlete.

Brittany Bowe

I grew up very much an athlete and very much a swimmer and a dancer and a horse rider and surf lifesaving club, you name it I've probably done it. I just find so much gratification in being physical.

Sharni Vinson

I think one has to understand that there are stages in life, and that the life of an athlete has its limits. It's short, and then it stops, and sooner or later you have to accept that.

David Nalbandian

It's a completely different thing, but there's so many things I learned from being an athlete that helped me in business. The only risk is not taking the risk. You've got to take that step.

Jaycie Phelps

I didn't train to make the Olympic team until 1968. I simply trained for the moment. I never even imagined I would be an Olympic athlete. It always seemed to evolve.

Dick Fosbury

You know, I always root for the older athlete. I root for the second album. I root for solo careers after the rock star breaks the band apart.

John Cho

My heroes, I couldn't imagine them practicing. Like Bob Dylan, you know? Bob Dylan's a very, very good guitar player, but it's like he's trying to hide it. I always loved this attitude. When you're very good... it's like being an athlete - and I always hated sports!

Laurent Brancowitz

I can't tell you why a particular athlete would leave a certain coach, but I can tell you there could be many reasons. They could have personality conflicts. They could have misunderstandings. Lots of stuff can happen.

Alberto Salazar

I was a professional athlete, the best baseball player in the world at one point.

Jose Canseco

Becoming an Olympian is the ultimate reward for any athlete.

Michael Diamond

Peterson was the most coachable athlete I have had in my life, and I coach many athletes.

Ato Boldon

You can't really describe how difficult it is to deal with. It is any athlete's worst nightmare to be accused of cheating by taking drugs. It really is very difficult to put into words how it makes you feel.

Greg Rusedski

I used to love to see Willie Pep and Ray Robinson. To me, the epitome of a great athlete is a great boxer. I just love the rhythm of seeing a man dance, slip punches. I loved the dancers and boxers. I would see them and be mesmerized.

Emanuel Steward

I like to push characters to extremes so they have to make really tough decisions and there is no life more extreme than that of an athlete.

Chris Cleave

Desire is the most important factor in the success of any athlete.

Bill Shoemaker

I started playing in '98, but I got hooked by playing celebrity golf tournaments. Tiger had a lot to do with it - his passion, the way that he plays. He's unique and different, and he inspired a lot of my passion. It's a sport you can't master. If you're an athlete, you can do almost anything, but golf is not like that.

Stuart Scott

My biggest accomplishment has been making a transition from athlete to author.

Kareem Abdul-Jabbar

As an athlete, you figure you work your whole life to have what you have, and to be able to show the world what you have and how proud you are of it, that's always fun.

Ricky Williams

I'm obviously always interested in the dancer who's an athlete and vice versa. I expect dancers to be in condition like an athlete is and to challenge themselves in the same way, to the same physical degree.

Twyla Tharp

I love what I do and I love being an athlete, but I also love all the things that have come with it.

Maria Sharapova

It's physically very, very, very trying to be onstage as a performer, not unlike an athlete, for thirty years.

Nikki Sixx

I had a client who was a professional baseball player once, and he would go to clubs and dance for seven, eight, nine hours at a time. He wouldn't drink, he wouldn't take drugs - he just danced because he had so much physical energy; he was this amazing athlete.

Martha Beck

You don't have to try to hurt people and be angry to be an athlete.

George Foreman

In high school and college, I was an athlete.

David Duchovny

I'm an athlete. I go out there and fight my heart out.

Maria Sharapova

I definitely feel like I'm more of an artist than an athlete. But I'm good at both.

Johnny Weir

I don't eat as much as an athlete should. I just don't like it.

Johnny Weir

When you are an athlete, it's difficult to take time off and say you want to come back without everyone judging you and attacking you.

Johnny Weir

There shouldn't be budget problems. There is so much money that goes untapped. If every athlete gave 5% of what they earned, there wouldn't be any budget problems.

George Foreman

I think an athlete should be honest. I know it's difficult, but if a guy knocked me on my can, I couldn't very well say, I slipped.

Sugar Ray Leonard

I have a real passion for children. I always wanted to teach and only became an athlete because my parents told my brother Parenthesis (sic) and me that we should use any God-given talent we had.

Gail Devers

People assume that because I'm a great athlete, I can dance. But no. My rhythm is off a little bit.

Jackie Joyner-Kersee

People assuming that because I'm a great athlete, I can dance. But no. My rhythm is off a little bit.

Jackie Joyner-Kersee

I've always looked at my career as an athlete would look at his. I won't play forever. Some don't know when to walk away, but the smart ones do.

Mark Wahlberg

I feel like at the Olympics I gave the best performance of my life and I wasn't rewarded for that as an athlete. Yes, my fans and my mom were happy about it, but I didn't win that gold medal.

Johnny Weir

I am much more of a geek than I am an athlete.

Curt Schilling

I still can't believe I'm an Olympic athlete.

Shawn Johnson

Tiger Woods makes me a better athlete.

Lindsey Vonn

On the court, Jason Collins is not a huge basketball star, but he has already claimed his place in civil rights history as the first openly gay athlete to play in one of the four major U.S. sports leagues.

Nancy Gibbs

I think it's ironic that I fell in love with a man I thought I would never be interested in because he's an athlete. I was always, 'An athlete? Heck no.'

Jessica Simpson

It's of very little importance to me that I was born gay. It doesn't make me a better athlete, it doesn't make me a stronger person, it doesn't really do anything to enhance my life. It's just something I was born with, the same as green eyes.

Johnny Weir

Before even Court Grip, I just wanted to be a part of a brand that I felt that listened to the athlete and really catered to the athlete, and gave us what we were looking for.

Dwyane Wade

I was an athlete when I was growing up.

Jeremy Renner

I'm not Carl Lewis the athlete any more. I'm growing into a new person with new interests and new goals.

Carl Lewis

As an athlete, there are advantages being with a team and getting regular physio.

Paula Radcliffe

Life's short, you know? Especially as an athlete. Your career is very short, and you use the opportunities that you have because you're not going to have them again.

Lindsey Vonn

I've been an athlete most of my life and on a disciplined schedule. Working out for me is just part of my every day.

Apolo Ohno

Arthur Ashe had been the first black athlete to play Johannesburg at the time of apartheid.

Yannick Noah

I'm never going to be an athlete, never going to be running triathlons - I'm not that person.

Jamie Lee Curtis

I started ballet in my early 20s. I studied for about ten years. Ballet is probably the one of the hardest things I've done, almost like MMA. People don't give it a lot of credit and think it's easy, but it's very difficult. For an athlete, you use muscles you really don't use, and ballet is something I really respect.

Herschel Walker

I think a great athlete transcends eras.

Dan Jenkins

I remember as a kid watching one of the Olympic games, and I was cheering for a big track athlete. He was the favorite to win, and he lost. I realized in that moment the pain he felt was so much greater than the pain that those who never thought they were going to win would have felt had they lost.

Malcolm Gladwell

Just as an athlete with natural gifts may fail to develop the fundamental skills necessary to play their sport after their talent fades, so people naturally disposed to faith may fail to develop the skills necessary to sustain them for a lifetime.

Stanley Hauerwas

I'm not an athlete dater, really. I would get too jealous. They're really gone all the time. Different hotel rooms.

Christine Teigen

As a child I wanted to be a professional athlete or lawyer.

Walter Dean Myers

When I was in high school I was a super serious athlete. I wasn't fun at all.

Seann William Scott

In front of the world, all of a sudden I'm a great athlete and I'm put into an environment with 25 other women and I'm expected to go to team meals, team functions.

Hope Solo

I want to break into the acting industry. It's something I have a great deal of respect for; it's a passion of mine. It's so amazing, the differences between acting and being an athlete, but the one commonality is they both evoke emotion in the viewer. And those emotions are real. So I think that's pretty cool.

Apolo Ohno

I've been a sports fan all my life, and like most other actors, I'm convinced I could have been a pro athlete if Hollywood hadn't come calling.

Jamie Foxx

An athlete and actor are really two different temperaments, night and day. As an athlete you really keep things out and as an actor you really bring things in.

Carl Lewis

I'm very serious about becoming a dramatic actor. I don't want to play cameo parts walking on as Carl Lewis the athlete. I want to go on stage or screen and be taken seriously.

Carl Lewis

Forty years ago the chances of journalists reporting - or the authorities even prosecuting - a pro athlete were practically nil.

Leigh Steinberg

To have any doubt in your body is the biggest weakness an athlete can have. There are times when I physically can't get myself to go for a skill because I'm thinking, 'My knee hurts really bad.'

Shawn Johnson

I was always a thin kid; I was an athlete.

Artie Lange

In 1981, I spoke at the Olympic Congress. I was scandalised that I was the first athlete to be given that chance. But I made the most of it.

Sebastian Coe

I missed being considered an athlete and having that competitive drive, and missed having something to work for every day. I'd taken two and a half years away from the sport and was out of shape. I wanted to get back to where I was in 2008.

Shawn Johnson

It's like being an athlete; you get into a certain shape where you really have the right wind, because it's all to do with breath. Because singing and dancing at the same time is not easy!

Liza Minnelli

I'm a golfer - not an athlete.

Lee Westwood

I was an athlete. And I proved I didn't win just because I was pretty. I was good, too.

Katarina Witt

The selfish thing about an athlete is you always look at the side of things where you say I could've done that better.

Andy Roddick

When you put the interest of a kid on money instead of heart then you're destroying the beauty of our lives and our thought process, which should be about how much responsibilities you carry as an athlete and a citizen.

Alexis Arguello

Growing up in Harlem, I had the chance to practice with a Negro League team. At fifteen, I was over six feet tall and a fair athlete, but my skills didn't come close to some of the players I saw.

Walter Dean Myers

People tend to like an athlete's performance, but if you don't get a feeling for the individual, you're not very emotive about them.

Daley Thompson

My father was a really good athlete, so his pop-ups really were sky high. Eventually I learned how to judge them properly and catch them well. It was great training for when I started to play on teams, which I did all through school.

Artie Lange

I think there's nothing sadder than a pro athlete who plays past his prime.

Lynn Samuels

Being in school is the best place to be if you are an athlete because you can structure your own time.

Frank Shorter

I used to be an athlete and even ran the 400 metre stretch for Tamil Nadu. I have always been active.

Arjun Rampal

I have to hit the gym. I have beauty appointments. I have to work toward my next job and maintaining my image, just like an athlete.

Linda Evangelista

I just want to continue the success and be an athlete that is shown in a good light in New York City.

Victor Cruz

The whole Miami Heat team is my least my favorite athlete. Why? Because they keep beating my Pacers.

Mike Epps

When I was playing I never wished I was doing anything else. I think being a professional athlete is the finest thing a man can do.

Bob Gibson

I am a National Football League player of American Samoan heritage. Because of my status as a professional athlete, I have been blessed to play a role in educating players and fans about the culture and history of America's southernmost territory.

Troy Polamalu

As a child, I wanted to be an athlete, a professional tennis player or something like that.

Jonathan Ames

A lot of people who watch figure skaters want us to look like pretty princesses. I want people to see the athlete, and I want to look like a woman among girls.

Ashley Wagner

When I was younger, I used to wrestle, and I feel that it contributed to my athletic ability because as a wrestler you have to be an all-encompassed athlete. You need stamina, strength, endurance and mental capacity. You also have to learn how to adapt in any situation.

Dhani Jones

As an athlete, you're brought up with that mentality that you finish everything you start. If you're going to start a meal, you're going to finish it until the plate is clean. I had to change that mentality to one of where, 'I eat until I'm full and leave the rest.'

Michael Strahan

When you're a 20-something-year-old athlete and you're getting a six-figure check every week, you're not thinking about next week. You're not thinking, 'I'm going to be broke,' or 'I'm going to need another job.' But I'll tell you, there are a lot of broke athletes out there - I know plenty - and I didn't want to end up as one.

Michael Strahan

You are an athlete when you're onstage. You can't get tired.

Faye Dunaway

I'm slightly influenced by sport in that I like the idea of trying, like an athlete, to keep absolutely ready. That's an emotional thing, almost. I don't mean physically, although I play tennis. But you try to keep yourself ready.

Colm Toibin

Once you start worrying about a national football championship, then you begin to worry about getting the quality of athlete, and the numbers needed, to win a national championship. And that worry leads to pressure to compromise academic standards to admit those athletes.

Derek Bok

The most important part of this is to prepare the athlete for life in general and then be able to compete.

Alberto Juantorena

I was an athlete growing up and I miss that. I miss hanging out with dudes and making raunchy jokes and telling stories, trading details, you know? There's something I really miss about that.

Chris Pratt

For me, I've lived a life as an athlete.

Giancarlo Esposito

I was afraid I would see someone from my past who thought I was this big athlete, and then I end up being just normal.

Victor Cruz

The irony of that is, what makes it kind of ironic, is when you do become successful as a professional athlete in particular, a lot of the young children who are emulating these stars do have a different perspective.

Frank Shorter

I was the very first athlete in East Germany allowed to go professional.

Katarina Witt

When you reach a certain level, you live in a bubble when all you think, dream and breathe is becoming the best athlete in the world.

Katarina Witt

People want athletes to cater to their image of what an athlete should be, but they also want them to fail so they can feel like their screwups are all right. If I make a priority shift, I'll make it because it's best for me.

Bode Miller

I grew up an athlete. Track and field and dance. In track, I actually went to the Junior Olympics. I've always been very athletic.

Kimberly Elise

To chase an athlete that really doesn't want to speak with you and when you finally get him, gives you three words and you have to write a story based on three words of information he gave you, that's pretty tough.

Junior Seau

I'm an athlete rep, so I'll be available if they need me for anything.

Shannon Miller

But at school, I wasn't athletic, and if you're not athlete in high school, it's kind of hard to find your place, so play practice seemed perfect, especially if you were as uncoordinated as I was.

Piper Perabo

I want to know about what makes an athlete tick.

Lisa Guerrero

I kind of rode this weird line between athlete and artist. It was a little different because most of the athletes were total jocks, and most of the artists dressed in black and were kind of considered a little on the fringe. But I hung out with both crowds in my high school.

Terry Crews

I was a sports nut. I stayed after school probably three hours every day - from fall, to winter, to spring. I went from football to basketball to track, and it started all over again. I loved all of it. I just loved being an athlete and all that it entailed. It really accounts for who I am today and even how I think today.

Terry Crews

I think I was a pretty selfish athlete.

Melanie Roach

I don't think of myself as an explorer but as an athlete.

Ben Saunders

I was a nerd academically. But I was also an athlete and a musician. I never wanted to be shut out of any situation. I think it was that more than anything.

Brian McKnight

As athletes, we're defined by what we've accomplished. Those are what most people remember and what you get paid for. But I learned more from my failures than from all of my successes put together - failures as an athlete and as a person.

Dan O'Brien

I always tried to hide the fact that I was an athlete. I just wanted to be normal.

Lindsay Davenport

I want to compete in the next Olympics. If I go to Rio, it will be my third time, which is a rare feat for an Indian athlete. For me, Olympics is important because it's the biggest event on earth for a sports person. I hope this time around I come back with a medal.

Vijender Singh

The moment an athlete doesn't train, things start to get a bit rusty.

Gareth Gates

Rosie knows how to play ball. She's an athlete, for sure.

Geena Davis

An athlete learns how to hold her breath, but that doesn't work in singing. You have to learn to relax.

Cathy Rigby

I was a judo athlete, while taking modeling as my side job, before I eventually quit my professional sports career over a knee injury.

Joe Taslim

It's that athlete's obsessiveness - the need to prove yourself and work harder than anybody else. I think it's what helped me do well in the theater.

Cathy Rigby

My parents wanted me to become a national athlete.

Joe Taslim

I think when you are the parents of a gifted athlete, the best thing in the world you can do is to encourage them, in my opinion. My dad didn't push me and I didn't push my children in athletics.

Bob Lilly

I did not choose necessarily on the basis of significance. If you have a vote for the most significant athlete, then you have Ali, then you have Babe Ruth, then you have Michael Jordan.

Dick Schaap

Tony knew me both as an athlete and as a person. He cared for me like a father.

Dennis Eckersley

As an athlete, you choose your sport and are drawn into it but your passion should never be driven by fame and fortune but a desire to create something special that people will always remember.

Katarina Witt

The concentration of the elite athlete is akin perhaps to the concentration of the writer.

Julia Leigh

I had a job on college campus. I lost that job, but on my way home I heard an inner voice that said go out for the baseball team. I was a walk-on, and I was actually petrified as a walk-on because you're not an athlete.

Lou Brock

In my opinion, Jackie is the greatest female athlete ever.

Marion Jones

I'm an athlete. I'm strong. I'm tough. And that's how women should be. That's how they should be built.

Bristol Palin

I just wanted to be an athlete.

Merlin Olsen

To an extreme athlete, there's a certain appeal to doing extreme things - seeking the most extreme physical challenges in some of the most extreme climates in the world. Testing and expanding the limits of human endurance is kind of my thing.

Dean Karnazes

Every NBA player, every athlete, I think once you get to this level in life, whether you have kids or you're about to have kids, understands that this is so much bigger than this sport.

Allan Houston

At one point that's all I cared about, being a pro athlete. But I realized I wasn't athletic enough.

Josh Duhamel

I learned a lot from my father. I'm very lucky to have a father who was a professional athlete.

Joakim Noah

I think being an athlete prepares you for more things than people give us credit for.

Eric Shanteau

Growing up, I wasn't an athlete or anything like that. The only place I felt like I belonged was in the theater.

Bobby Cannavale

The Madden NFL franchise holds a special place in popular culture and the cover is a coveted position for players all over the league. I'm honored to be the first cover athlete chosen by

Madden NFL fans and it's a great way to cap off an amazing year for the Saints and the city of New Orleans.

Drew Brees

I think no athlete wants to end his career on an injury.

Jayson Williams

Coaches know that a parent publicly scolding his kid after a race will not help the athlete perform better.

Don Kardong

Support the athlete, encourage the team, help the coach. That's what good track parents do.

Don Kardong

Israel is one of the easiest places to play ball. When I say easy I am referring to the easy lifestyle an athlete has while in Israel. It's very easy to get around the country, because it's so small.

Michael Kennedy

When first starting to work with someone you try to get them in the same mindset that you were in when you were successful, and I realized the best thing you can ever do is realize that they are not you. They have a different persona and mindset, and you have to figure out what works best within your communication with that athlete.

Dan O'Brien

You are an athlete if you are a dancer.

Sharon Lawrence

Beside the brand-ambassador elements of the modern racing driver, the evolution of the athlete has mandated that as drivers, we are very committed to fitness.

Charlie Kimball

My life as a professional athlete has allowed me the opportunity to visit and live in many different places and meet many interesting and diverse people.

Scott Pruett

As an athlete, I was never really comfortable with being a celebrity.

Michael Johnson

I used to go to some Harvard parties with my athlete friends, and they would introduce me as 'Winona, the Indian activist.' It made me uncomfortable. I felt like a novelty.

Winona LaDuke

I love sports. I was an athlete in high school, and my school was so small we didn't have a football team, so it's the one sport I didn't bother to learn the rules to because I never went to game.

Katie Aselton

I think the two most important parts of any athlete's workouts are his leg workouts and his core training.

Albert Pujols

I was probably in the best shape of any athlete at the time, but you don't get to pass judgment on yourself.

Steve Carlton

I was fully immersed in the now as an athlete.

Kyle Shewfelt

But now - look, I have to take care of myself. I work out every day. I'm a dancer. I've always been an athlete, and I'm one of those people who start to go crazy if they don't run or do something.

Vanessa Carlton

Being on TV is similar to being an athlete. You get no second chances.

Lara Spencer

I'm a different athlete, I'm a different person.

Libby Trickett

I really didn't realise until I got back the work that goes into a performance. You're like an athlete - if you haven't been practising things tighten up. I had to do a lot of practice work, but I got through it. Even when I was 21 I would have a 40-minute nap on the day of a show, and I will still do that.

Michael Crawford

He has a method that likens the musician to an athlete, so I do physical exercises designed to keep a musician in shape in order to perform the function, which is to play music.

Herb Alpert

It probably won't sink in until I've retired from running but I'm a much better athlete than two years ago.

Michael East

As an athlete, you sort of just win every day. Because you're going to sometimes lose every day. And so you just keep picking yourself up and going forward.

Beth Brooke

When I'm in the gym, I'm in the gym, and that is my focus. But when I'm not in the gym, I'm enjoying being a mom and taking care of those responsibilities .. They really do provide me with the balance that I need to be a more complete athlete.

Melanie Roach

I'm still an athlete, I'm still a stockbroker, I'm still an actor. I think of it as more of an opening of new doors than an actual transition. I enjoy all of those things, which is why they remain a part of my life.

Brian J. White

My favorite athlete of all time would have to be Jim Thorpe.

Randy Castillo

Madonna is an athlete; she has to be treated like a professional athlete. She doesn't work out for six hours a day, though, like some of the press says. She never works out for more than two hours a day, and then only when she has the time.

Tracy Anderson

For an athlete myself, it is especially meaningful for our country to host an Olympics. Every athlete hopes to participate in an Olympics, so I still can't believe the games of dreams is going to take place in Korea.

Yuna Kim

Also, to be honest, my dad wanted me to be an athlete. And I think all sons want to prove something to their dad. So now, aged 35, I want to see what I can achieve physically.

Joe Manganiello

Being an athlete in a cold-weather sport is really difficult to deal with the asthma.

Charlie White

Never played football, but I'm an athlete. I'm a competitor.

Michael B. Jordan

The Olympic Games are always in the head of every sports athlete. We work for that.

Tina Maze

As an athlete, when you have a desire and a want to do something, you fight for it. And it doesn't matter how long your journey is; it's whether you give up or don't.

Troy Dumais

Female success stories from sporting events like the Olympic Games have played a role in shifting the Indian perception to see the female athlete as a hero and a role model for young Indian girls.

Richard Attias

If I could change on thing about myself, I would: Have better knees. Mine are shot because of injuries. You're only as good as your legs, whether you're an athlete or an actor.

William Petersen

I'm in the gym three to four days a week, depending on how I'm feeling. With chest, legs and back being the most important parts of any athlete's body, I try to train these on separate days with at least a day off in between.

Albert Pujols

I'm continuing to prepare very well because I have my responsibility and my (pride) as a man and an athlete.

Dayron Robles

I remember making the all-star team in Little League when I was around 11 years old. I was not a great athlete, but I loved it, so making starting second base in the all-star was great for me. I think someone must have been sick and they slotted me in.

Ralph Macchio

If you're a professional athlete, and after the game, you're eating at the same place that somebody in the audience is eating at? You're making a mistake.

John Salley

I always wanted to be a professional athlete. I love my life.

Billy Horschel

I'm an athlete, so I'm very interested in making the sport as safe as possible - just for my own career longevity.

Ted Ligety

I'm an athlete, but I'm not a runner. I'm 5-foot-8 and stocky - not exactly a runner's type.

Andrew Lawrence

I always wanted to be an athlete. Then when I realized that I can't run very fast, jump very high, or catch anything, I thought, 'Maybe if this doesn't work out, I can be an actor.'

Geoff Stults

I like to think of myself as a pretty good athlete, I don't think I'm a great sprinter, but 200, 400, maybe 800. I won't say excel in them, but I'd do pretty good.

Grant Hill

It's a fine balance for an athlete in enjoying the moment and being really satisfied, say, with a run, and with your day, and knowing you can make it better in the future.

Hannah Kearney

My background is that of a competitive athlete and a fighter, and I'm bringing something totally different to 'The Biggest Loser' that wasn't there before.

Cara Castronuova

I really feel like that concept of enjoying the now and not worrying about the future is what my coach has been trying to teach me for 14 years - and that is what has made me such a different athlete 10 years later, and that is what has made me strong enough mentally to make this Olympic team.

Melanie Roach

I was an athlete growing up. I did a lot of sports: soccer, basketball, so I was always so used to hardcore training, a lot of running. I got to a point where I felt like I just wanted to get toned; I didn't need to shed pounds, so now I do Pilates.

Jacquelyn Jablonski

The CrossFit program is broad, general and inclusive, and most of all, the movements can be scaled down to any level of athlete. Just watch what I do with it on 'The Biggest Loser.'

Bob Harper

The shortstop is a perfectly conditioned athlete. You're running out on relays all the time. You're covering second base. On every pitch, you're moving.

Lou Boudreau

I'm probably the least flexible athlete you'll find. When it comes to yoga, I can't get in the positions and I can't hold them. You have to be pretty flexible to do it. Once you get certain positions, you have to have the core strength to hold those positions. It's a pretty good workout.

Steve Blake

I'm very involved in Shred, constantly checking in on something. It takes a lot of time. But it has let me leverage who I am as an athlete into a product.

Ted Ligety

I've always felt I should do things 100 percent or not do them. It's all or nothing. That's what makes me a good athlete - doing things with all the 'ganas' I can.

Sergio Garcia

I really didn't have one particular athlete I liked growing up.

Masahiro Tanaka

I would say that one of the really special gifts about playing an athlete is that it's the best motivation you'll ever have to get in top shape and stay in top shape because you know that you're going to be expected to deliver.

Holt McCallany

I just see myself as an athlete and a competitor, someone who just works really hard at trying to get better at golf.

Zach Johnson

I've found that there's a lot to invigorate in any country or destination - it's all about how you look at it. I've never really had any difficulties anywhere I've been. As an athlete, I used to enjoy being on the road and meeting people.

Bob Beamon

When I was a kid, I had serious athlete's foot and nosebleeds.

Ken Kercheval

You don't have to look like an Under Armour mannequin to be an athlete. A lot of people probably think I'm not athletic or don't even try to work out or whatever, but I do. Just because you're big doesn't mean you can't be an athlete. And just because you work out doesn't mean you're going to have a 12-pack.

Prince Fielder

Any athlete has massive reserves in their body and their emotional landscape.

Edoardo Ponti

There aren't too many principles of proper business conduct with which just about everybody will agree. Two come to mind: 1. Unless you're a professional athlete, don't offer co-workers encouragement by patting them on the butt, and 2. Don't burn bridges.

Dale Dauten

Everyone probably says this, but my favorite athlete is Tony Hawk. I'd really love to meet him.

Mason Cook

I enjoy sports, and love being involved in any outdoor sport from volleyball to softball. I'm not being immodest when I say I'm a natural athlete.

Ginger Rogers

When I go through the airport and see white women walking through the airport barefooted, like athlete's feet don't exist, there's something wrong.

Dick Gregory

I love athletics. As an athlete, I like to believe I can still do the things I used to do when I was once young.

Dominique Dawes

I think every athlete has their window of opportunity, and you just have to jump on it. You never know when it can end. So I'm just trying to live large while I have the opportunity.

Hope Solo

Carl Yastrzemski was the best all-around player. He could run, throw and hit. He had the ability to play a number of different positions. He signed as a shortstop. He could play the outfield, of course, and third base and first, too. He was a tremendous athlete. Mickey Mantle was unbelievable, too.

Al Kaline

I mean, as an athlete, as a competitor, you have to have that belief in yourself.

Tiger Woods

I think every athlete will tell you no matter what sport you're in, when you train so hard and when you care so much about doing what you do, there's a little bit of nerves that come with that. But nerves that won't prevent you form performing, nerves that, hopefully, allow you to be that much more motivated and inspired to do well.

Sidney Crosby

I'm proud of the way I've dealt with setbacks. It's hard when you feel down and you think, 'Why is the world doing this to me?' But you have to pick yourself up again. That's what makes you a better athlete.

Jessica Ennis

One of the reasons I connect to the Super Bowl is that I approach my shows like an athlete.

Beyonce Knowles

You're a person a lot longer before and after you're a professional athlete. People always say to me, 'Your image is this, your image is that.' Your image isn't your character. Character is what you are as a person. That's what I worry about.

Derek Jeter

To be a top-class athlete, you have to train hard, you have to eat right, you have to get enough rest. I feel the way golf is going nowadays, you have to treat yourself as an athlete.

Rory McIlroy

You see a hockey player, you'd never know he's a professional athlete. But you put the skates on him, and he becomes a beast.

Junior Seau

You can't be a creative thinker if you're not stimulating your mind, just as you can't be an Olympic athlete if you don't train regularly.

Ken Robinson

America believes in education: the average professor earns more money in a year than a professional athlete earns in a whole week.

Evan Esar

I don't think some athletes understand how big it is to be an athlete, what they can do with just a simple gesture of shaking a kid's hand. It can make a fan's day. It can make a fan's life.

Matt Kemp

There's no question that O.J. Simpson had been a substitute white man in America. He had gained honorary white status. He was not viewed by many white Americans as black. He was not seen as the African American athlete who was rebellious: Jim Brown, Muhammad Ali, Hank Aaron... He was accepted in golf clubs that were very tony.

Michael Eric Dyson

I'm really clear about what my life mission is now. There's no more depression or lethargy, and I feel like I've returned to the athlete I once was. I'm integrating all the parts of me - jock, musician, writer, poet, philosopher - and becoming stronger as a result.

Alanis Morissette

Don't live vicariously through your kids or try to shape them into who you wanted to be, like the popular kid or an athlete. Children should be given the opportunity to be themselves.

Joan Cusack

I don't know why people question the academic training of an athlete. Fifty percent of the doctors in this country graduated in the bottom half of their classes.

Al McGuire

When you speak of role models, when we talk to our kids, everybody is a role model, everyone, just as you look at a Michael Jordan to be the terrific athlete he is.

Walter Payton

I find it funny how people from Boston and New York hate each other because of pro teams. But, like, everyone on the Red Sox is a random millionaire athlete from somewhere else.

Julian Casablancas

An athlete must have ability to reach the top, but many who have ability and who do not live clean lives never have and never will be champions for obvious reasons.

Major Taylor

You look at a Pete Rose to be the terrific athlete he is and then he falls on hard times, but when he played the game, I got something from the way he played the game because he hustled every play, and just because he had one mistake in his life, am I supposed to throw back everything that I gained from him?

Walter Payton

The young athlete who aspires to greatness, generally speaking, learns a number of things from several different coaches. The first one taught him the fundamentals; the second one instilled discipline in him and taught him more of the techniques that must be mastered to excel.

Zig Ziglar

It's tough to be a 15- or 16-year-old athlete competing around the country. There's tension, there's media. I had no idea what I was getting into.

Lance Armstrong

When I found Jesus Christ, I learned to be a better athlete. I didn't have to go out there and knock them out in the first round. I've learned to be patient, skillful in the ring. At the same time, I wanted to prove to other boxers that you can take off this killer instinct stuff, you can be a great athlete, a great boxer, and love your brother.

George Foreman

I change my socks often, because I had bad bouts of athlete's foot fungus infections as a kid. I may be able to change socks less frequently and not get the fungus. But, I'd rather not run the test to determine just how infrequently I could change socks. I don't feel superstitious about it.

Bill Nye

Thank you to everyone that has made me the athlete I am! God, family and friends, my competitors and supporters! You have all had a hand!

Oscar Pistorius

Durability is part of what makes a great athlete.

Bill Russell

Success for an athlete follows many years of hard work and dedication.

Michael Diamond

If you're an athlete and you completely focus on the body, you're missing other components. Similarly, if you're trying to broaden your mind but not also being attentive to your sense of humour and your spirit, then you're not going to grow and develop so fast.

Aimee Mullins

I want to be remembered as a great athlete. As a boxing champion.

Idi Amin

If you don't eat right as an athlete, you'll get tired and won't be as sharp. It's simple to drink sodas and sports drinks, but water is the most essential drink to put in your body.

Troy Polamalu

The U.S. Olympic spirit award is an award that is given to an athlete who embodies the Olympic spirit in more ways than just on the playing field, in showing incredible perseverance, in overcoming obstacles, and what we wanted to do is have everybody can vote on-line.

Brian Boitano

I don't want to get too detailed into it, but when you're a good high school running back, you can almost be whatever type of runner you want to be. If you're a good size and a good athlete, you can be whatever type of runner you want.

Barry Sanders

You know raising a family in the lifestyle of a professional athlete can be very difficult.

Robin Yount

Growing up in Huntington Beach, you were either a traditional sports athlete, a skateboarder, or a surfer. I got my first skateboard when I was five and skated off and on over the years, did a little BMX racing as a kid, and then in my freshman or sophomore year I started getting a little bit more into skateboarding.

Jason Lee

Developing the muscles of the soul demands no competitive spirit, no killer instinct, although it may erect pain barriers that the spiritual athlete must crash through.

Germaine Greer

Fatigue makes fools of us all. It robs you of your skills and your judgment, and it blinds you to creative solutions. It's the best-conditioned athlete, not the most talented, who generally wins when the going gets tough.

Harvey Mackay

The actor becomes an emotional athlete. The process is painful - my personal life suffers.

Al Pacino

I think there is no better way to invite a human being to view their body differently than by inviting them to be an athlete, by revering one's body as an instrument rather than just an ornament.

Alanis Morissette

In the marathon a crazy athlete can just keep pushing from the beginning, at a championship you don't need a time just to win the race.

Haile Gebrselassie

My brother David was a great athlete and I knew there was no way I could live up to that.

Billie Joe Armstrong

We thought I was going to be a great athlete, and we were wrong, and I thought I was going to be a great entertainer, and that wasn't it either. I'm going to be an American Citizen. First class.

Dick Gregory

I'm not just a model who plays volleyball, or a volleyball player who supports herself modeling. I'm a female athlete personality.

Gabrielle Reece

You can wish as hard as you like but all that really matters is the shape you're in on the day of the race. I've always felt these really big races aren't necessarily won by whoever is the fastest. They're won by the athlete who is the smartest and in the best shape on the day.

Paula Radcliffe

The Olympics is about showing what you've done with your life, your dream as an athlete and sharing that with the world.

Sasha Cohen

The athlete of today is not an athlete alone. He's the center of a team - doctors, scientists, coaches, agents and so on.

Emil Zatopek

I'm an athlete and I'm black, and a lot of black athletes go broke. I do not want to become a statistic, so maybe I overcompensate. But I'm paranoid. Oprah told me a long time ago, 'You sign every check. Never let anyone sign any checks.'

Serena Williams

Good ideas are like Nike sports shoes. They may facilitate success for an athlete who possesses them, but on their own they are nothing but an overpriced pair of sneakers. Sports shoes don't win races. Athletes do.

Felix Dennis

I'm an athlete, so I can dress down with the best of them. I can throw on t-shirts and sweats with the best of them.

Dwyane Wade

I think nowadays it's so easy as an athlete to become a statistic whether or not you lose everything or having trouble or whatever it may be.

Venus Williams

Acting is a bit like being an athlete. You spend all your time getting ready to do something for two minutes. All the things that made my career in the movies happen took two or three minutes, which is the time that it takes for a 'take'. In that time, something happens. That's what people know you for, just like someone running the hundred metres.

Christopher Walken

At the end of the day, if you're a professional athlete in track and field you are the CEO of your company.

Carl Lewis

Every athlete acquires routines as a way to help control nerves.

Hope Solo

It is the inspiration of the Olympic Games that drives people not only to compete but to improve, and to bring lasting spiritual and moral benefits to the athlete and inspiration to those lucky enough to witness the athletic dedication.

Herb Elliott

The conditioning and the lifestyle changes you have to make to remain a healthy athlete are what molded me into what I am today.

John Cena

My biggest weakness as a endurance athlete has been in not drinking enough water after training, thereby racing sometimes while dehydrated.

Bill Rodgers

Even though I'm not a competitive athlete, I have to still maintain things and try to keep myself fit because I am at that age where I need to make sure to get those regular checkups and make sure everything is in tact.

Jackie Joyner-Kersee

In 2008 I didn't take it all in enough. I was so wrapped up in just the competition that I missed what was going on around me. If I am given that opportunity again to go to the Olympics and be an athlete I want to take it all in because I feel like this is my last shot and I want to feel the team spirit. I want to really live and breathe the USA.

Shawn Johnson

If you got anything to you at all as an athlete and a competitor, you don't care what the circumstances are. You still got competition.

Bill Parcells

I don't think there is a perfect athlete. But if I had to come close to picking someone who demonstrates all the traits that I feel an athlete should have, I would say the perfect athlete would be Tiger Woods. He has the ability, he's humble and he's very good at what he does.

Jackie Joyner-Kersee

I was a total athlete. I loved sports, but when I realized I wasn't going to be a professional athlete, I realized I wanted to be in movies.

Seann William Scott

As an athlete, you only have so much time. The window only has so much time and then it closes. You have to take care of yourself the best you can.

Barry Bonds

I found the emotion that as an athlete you block out, and it really helped me to understand myself as a person. I'm a really emotional person and it helped make me a better person.

Carl Lewis

I can play basketball, run track, and play volleyball, so yeah, I've always been an athlete at heart.

Vivica A. Fox

I always said I wanted to be a great athlete, ever since I was an overweight little kid. I just love competing in any kind of athletics.

Herschel Walker

All my life I believed I became an athlete through my own determination, but it's impossible to think that being descended from slaves hasn't left an imprint through the generations.

Michael Johnson

There were only 170 neurologists in Britain then and, whether spoken or unspoken, there was this insidious feeling. How can Bannister, a mere athlete, probably spoilt by all the publicity and fame, dare aspire to neurology? But I'd done a lot of research, and my academic record was very good.

Roger Bannister

I was always a mean and lean athlete - not tall - not large.

Edwin Moses

When you're an athlete and you play every day and are conditioning yourself every year, the aging is gradual.

Cal Ripken, Jr.

The nearest approach I have ever seen to the symmetry of ancient sculpture was among the Arab tribes of Ethiopia. Our Saxon race can supply the athlete, but not the Apollo.

Bayard Taylor

Growing up, I started developing confidence in what I felt. My parents helped me to believe in myself. I wasn't the best looking guy, I wasn't the best athlete in the world, but they made me feel good about myself.

Herschel Walker

The pro athlete is a sad tale. He signs a big contract and thinks he's set for life. I didn't think I was set for life, and I don't now. As athletes, we are important, celebrities, in demand and rich. Then we are out of the game and we are not important, not celebrities, not in demand and not rich.

Fran Tarkenton

There has never been a great athlete who died not knowing what pain is.

Bill Bradley

Paul Robeson was an athlete, Rutgers valedictorian, lawyer, writer, actor in movies and plays, great voice - a black male doing it all, back when some people thought he shouldn't. One reason I do all the things I do is to break stereotypes that people can only do certain things.

Dhani Jones

Muhammad Ali is a combination of personality and athlete who is probably better known around the world than any other. He became a great hero.

Will McDonough

Being an athlete, you try to get protein.

Ronda Rousey

Being an athlete, you know how to train and prepare your body for a performance and you're able to do it under pressure.

Kristi Yamaguchi

As a young athlete, it was first about having fun; then it was about winning.

Dan O'Brien

I was an athlete growing up. I was a wrestler, I played football, so I can take a fall. I actually wanted to be a stuntman when I was kid, so I would practice falling down the stairs. It's just something I like to do.

Chris Pratt

Honestly, it's not the medals that I feel so proud of. It's the way I conducted myself as an athlete, the hard work that I put forward.

Kyle Shewfelt

Passion and hunger are the two ingredients that I look for in first making the judgment on - whether an athlete, an assistant coach, or a horse trainer or anybody I do business with.

Rick Pitino

Like every other athlete, I always dreamt of playing at the Olympics, and it feels really good to see that dream materialize.

Mary Kom

Every professional athlete owes a debt of gratitude to the fans and management, and pays an installment every time he plays. He should never miss a payment.

Bobby Hull

Everybody doesn't get to do each and every film. I don't compete with others; I compete with myself. I have been an athlete, a sportsperson; so I know how to be competitive in a healthy way.

Deepika Padukone

Acting is sort of an extension of childhood. You get to play all of these roles and have so much fun. Playing an athlete would be so cool. Or where you get to shoot guns, ride horses. I wouldn't turn down any of that.

Jon Hamm

I'm not a wushu champion. I was an athlete when I was a kid. I was a swimmer and a runner, but all this action stuff is such a challenge. It really, really is.

Maggie Q

I'm not going to relate to an athlete as a peer.

Lisa Guerrero

My thing about looking good is that it should be the character. If I'm playing a character who's concerned about his body - an athlete, say - I'll get in shape. If I'm playing a character who doesn't or wouldn't, I don't. I almost never get in shape for a movie, even though I know it would be a good career move.

Aidan Quinn

Do you need to train two hours a day? Probably not. The reason why my celebrity clients have to train two hours a day is because their endurance level is so strong. For Madonna to get results and keep results, it's like a professional athlete training - she has to push harder.

Tracy Anderson

It is not the time spent with the child at their activity that is going to produce the highest level athlete. It is in supporting the child in an organized activity - and Bill alluded to this - so the child can find what they truly like to do and let them go.

Frank Shorter

And as a true athlete, mistakes haunt you forever.

Jim Otto

All my life I believed I became an athlete through my own determination, but it's impossible to think that being descended from slaves hasn't left an imprint through the generations. Difficult as it was to hear, slavery has benefited descendants like me - I believe there is a superior athletic gene in us.

Michael Johnson

I like to think of the world's greatest athlete coming up to bat against me - Tiger Woods, Wayne Gretzky, I don't care who it is - and I'm looking at him thinking, you have no chance.

David Cone

There are some good teachers out there, but the only one who is a genius at diagnosing my swing is my mom. She took up golf late, when she was 39, but in her younger days, she was an amazing athlete. She never read an instruction book or took lessons, but she has a remarkable eye for motion.

Boo Weekley

It's like an athlete. He has a string of hot years, and then he fades into nothingness. The actor doesn't necessarily fade into nothingness. After his hot years, he fades into a different category.

Ed Asner

It's not just the physical aspect of boxing, it's the whole fighter mentality that has been ingrained in me through the years as a competitive athlete. One of the hardest things you'll ever do is to box - to get into the ring and to face off with somebody whose whole goal is to knock you out, to hurt you, and to be able to fight back.

Cara Castronuova

I like to be just an athlete, but if I go to competition and compete, I love to be a star, maybe.

Yuna Kim

Things have changed so much, with Facebook and Twitter. Everyone is so much more accessible these days: no British athlete has ever experienced what we are experiencing now. It's such a unique situation with the home Olympics.

Jessica Ennis

It's not my place to tell you whom to vote for, to take any political stand, to tell you what religion to believe in. I'm an athlete. I can influence certain things, but when I see other athletes and celebrities telling you whom to vote for, I actually get a bit offended.

Pete Sampras

I'm working on a movie called 'Labor Day' with Kate Winslet while still balancing kite boarding. Being an actress and an athlete is a challenge, but I'm excited to see what happens.

Maika Monroe

I used to bring my sketchbook to gym class and doodle, because I am a very uncoordinated athlete.

Kate Voegele

I am much more wired to be an athlete than anything else. I understand the 'hard work = payoff' equation in sports. I run marathons and I box. And that's my Puerto Rican flag hanging in Freddie Roach's Wild Card Boxing gym. I gave it to him. My last N.Y.C. marathon time I ran in three hours flat.

Kirk Acevedo

The most important thing for any athlete is to know his ability. If you know your ability and have even a little bit of a strong mindset, you can get success, because your ability takes you to success.

Virender Sehwag

As we all know, when you're an athlete things are a little bit easier for you. It didn't mean that what was going on inside my heart wasn't a bit of a thunderstorm, but outwardly I got along ok. I was really shy in seventh grade.

Stephen Chbosky

I think the people who have really followed my career from the time I was seven years old can see my steady progress and see the type of person and athlete I am.

Marion Jones

As a professional athlete, I believe that I need to explore my opportunities to the maximum, in order to excel and continue to play the best football I can.

Hidetoshi Nakata

Maybe there's a little girl who thinks she can be an Olympic athlete, and she sees all the things I struggled through to get here. Yeah, I didn't walk away with a medal or run away with a medal, but I think there's lessons to be learned when you win and lessons to be learned when you lose.

Lolo Jones

When an athlete has relegated the persistent rumors of cheating to the back room of the mind, he hasn't really forgotten them. And when he glances back to where rumors hunker in the darkness, he hopes with a savage heart that somehow, some day, those cheaters will be brought to justice.

Don Kardong

As a little kid, not only is my dad Jo-Jo White, but M. L. Carr is involved in the family, Red Auerbach is my godfather, and my stepmother was an Olympic-caliber sprinter. Athletes were all around. I happened to be a natural athlete. If I wasn't, it might have been hell. But I never got any pressure from my mom and dad to be an athlete.

Brian J. White

Some of today's athletes do not have that kind of pride. They left school at 16, have never had a job in their life and are getting Lottery funding, earning money as an athlete.

Linford Christie

At the very beginning of my career, when I opened my business in Italy, I was also a ranked tennis player. I had won many tournaments. To be an athlete was my first choice. Second choice: designer. However! There was more money in being a designer at that time.

Oleg Cassini

I was an only child of a father who loved me deeply, but we didn't play catch, even though I was an athlete. We didn't go fishing or hunting or any of the things I wanted to do. Why not? He just didn't do that.

Charlie Rose

Collin Jackson was a little before my time and he was a really good athlete. I've raced with him, but he's now retired. He's a really good role model and someone that I've learnt a lot from.

Liu Xiang

So while you're an athlete, and you have that platform, what you want to be able to do is make it work for you as much as possible, because there's going to be life after sports.

Stedman Graham

As an athlete, success is not just about winning; it is about working hard and giving it all you have. I have always taken one match at a time and worked hard; when I succeeded, I worked further on the aspects of the game which worked for me; when I failed, I listed out my weaknesses and worked on them.

Rohan Bopanna

If a female is good-looking, it totally decreases her credibility. Now she's not a good athlete - she's only good in these track meets because she's good-looking.

Lolo Jones

I was a terrible athlete and a pretty bad student. I couldn't focus. My imagination was always racing.

Lisi Harrison

I tell you, it was kind of two-fold. I fortunately had a lot of support. My coach was amazing - he told me to focus on being prepared and that is what I did. Every athlete is nervous - any athlete who tells you they're not nervous isn't telling you the truth. I was as prepared as I could be.

Carl Lewis

I'm a realist and I always have been. Quality training is what I do now; before it was a combination of both quality and quantity. Now I'm not trying to be a world-class athlete, I don't need to train at that level. It's about being fit, fit for life.

Jackie Joyner-Kersee

There's far more that goes into being a professional athlete than being a college athlete. So many differences that people don't realize. It's not just about playing football and getting paid to do it. There's a lot of things that you have to deal with.

Robert Griffin III

As an athlete, I've always been very proud to represent the United States.

Michelle Kwan

The first time I walked into the Olympic athlete village seeing the Visa ATM machine with my picture on it and the Chinese characters saying 'Destiny.' For some reason, it just boosted my confidence and it was before I had even worked out or had my first training or competed.

Nastia Liukin

I have no physical genius about me. I can't dribble a ball and run at the same time, I can't do lay-ups - I'm not an athlete. But my experience as a kid was, I was made fun of so much that what I did then, is, I wouldn't participate. And I think I cheated myself out of a lot of fun.

Rich Mullins

I used to pray that God would make me a great athlete, and He never did.

Lou Holtz

Had I been a great athlete, I'm not sure I would have even gone into coaching. I may have turned out feeling that my life ended when my athletic career ended, as happens so many times with various athletes.

Lou Holtz

Jackie Robinson, as an athlete and as someone who was trying to make a stand for equality, he was exemplary.

Kareem Abdul-Jabbar

OK, I'll put it like this: I doubt if we will see another All-American basketball athlete who is a Rhodes Scholar.

Kareem Abdul-Jabbar

With any kind of artistic thing, it's a muscle, like any athlete, and the moment you're not doing it, you lose all confidence. That's why I'm terrible with down time.

Daniel Radcliffe

Ask any athlete: We all hurt at times. I'm asking my body to go through seven different tasks. To ask it not to ache would be too much.

Jackie Joyner-Kersee

I hate divers, like Cristiano Ronaldo, who might be the greatest athlete in the sport, but he's a big baby. If things are going well he's great, but when things are going badly it's the ref's fault, it's his teammates' fault.

Viggo Mortensen

The activity of a singer that sings opera is similar to that of an athlete.

Andrea Bocelli

I still have so much passion to perform... That's who Johnny Weir is: I'm a figure skater, I'm an athlete. I want to have fun and enjoy it.

Johnny Weir

I always thought of myself as some sort of athlete until I started playing golf a couple years ago.

James Caan

A revised schedule is to business what a new season is to an athlete or a new canvas to an artist.

Norman Ralph Augustine

I have a real passion for children. I always wanted to teach and only became an athlete because my parents told my brother Parenthesis and me that we should use any God-given talent we had.

Gail Devers

The main thing about Bruce Lee is that, he was a little guy. And you know, his quickness, his aggressiveness, his explosive power, you have to be a great athlete to have all these, his body, his look, you know, all these things have to do with discipline and structure. He was able to go against the biggest guy, regardless of who he was.

Evander Holyfield

I would always love to be an athlete, but it's got to be a tough day when you have to hang up those cleats.

Kevin James

I wouldn't say I'm a phenomenon, just a great athlete.

Usain Bolt

The great thing about having a pool in L.A. is that I can use it year-round. And since I've always been an athlete, staying fit is very important.

Vera Wang

An opera singer is like an athlete before a match. An athlete cannot overdo anything. In order to perform at the highest possible level, you need to refrain from activities so as to be able to express this power.

Andrea Bocelli

I think I've gotten more attention after the Olympics than any other U.S. athlete, and it's really great that people are recognizing who I am and what I do. You look at Shaq and you see a basketball player. You look at Tiger Woods and you see a golfer. But people are responding to who I am.

Johnny Weir

The life of an athlete does have to be lonely and you have to be focused on your craft and what you do. Loneliness is just a sacrifice you make as an Olympic-level athlete.

Johnny Weir

I'm not the athlete I was when I was training for the Olympics in '92 or when I was working out every single day. I have to live in moderation: I work out three or four days a week, and I smile while I'm working out - I really do enjoy it. I work out with my girlfriends and make it a social competition.

Summer Sanders

An athlete gets paid a lot of money. And someone who is after that, a thief, a mugger or someone who steals from people, they are taking a chance with the law that if they get caught, they are going to jail or face some other problem. In my case, you are going to get shot.

Luke Scott

It's always a dream to be on the cover, it's one of the things an athlete always aspires to do, to be on the cover of a videogame, but I never thought I would get to do it this quick.

Dwyane Wade

The greatest feeling of accomplishment for me is the fact that I was an athlete who was somewhat disabled.

Bill Toomey

I don't know if I'm a good kickball player; I know I'm a good athlete.

Ryan Lochte

There is no correlation between a childhood success and a professional athlete.

Carl Lewis

So much of a professional athlete's success depends upon not necessarily the play itself but how he deals with... always saying how you deal with good, is just as important as how you deal with bad.

Brett Favre

The doors fly open when you're a professional athlete.

Dennis Rodman

Quality training is what I do now; before it was a combination of both quality and quantity. Now I'm not trying to be a world-class athlete, I don't need to train at that level. It's about being fit, fit for life.

Jackie Joyner-Kersee

Growing up as an athlete, I started skating very young. My parents didn't know anything about the sport, so they went with the flow. I had two great coaches who gave great advice and gave guidelines for my parents. My parents let the coaches dictate what was going on on the ice.

Kristi Yamaguchi

Records are the only thing that remain of an athlete, the only thing that people will remember. If I want to ensure that people don't forget me, I can only stop once I've set the bar as high as possible for anyone coming after me.

Lindsey Vonn

I never look backwards. I have always been an athlete. I boxed before I acted.

Mickey Rourke

I'm fortunate that my job gives me the motivation to be as fit as possible. I wound up in a profession that requires physical and mental preparation, so I get to prepare like an athlete for everything I do. I'm living the dream, man.

Mark Wahlberg

For an athlete, there's no time off... until it's over.

Terry Bradshaw

The paradox of endurance sports is that an athlete can never work as hard as he wants, because if he pushes himself too far, his hematocrit will fall.

Malcolm Gladwell

Every Olympic athlete prepares differently. For me, I am 100 percent into the sport. And if I decide to really make a crucial career decision to say, 'This is something I want to do,' I want to leave no stone unturned in my preparation.

Apolo Ohno

For an athlete, the biggest pressure comes from within. You know what you want to do and what you're capable of.

Paula Radcliffe

The Olympic Games were created for the exhaltation of the individual athlete.

Pierre de Coubertin

Being a pro athlete doesn't mean you treat your body right, even though it's so important to what you do. Being a runner and training for important races has taught me more about how to fuel than swimming ever did. I realize it's a process and part of the commitment.

Summer Sanders

Jim Thorpe is someone I've always loved. He was an Olympic athlete, you know, and a football player from back in the day. I'd love to play him. And then there's a guy called Iceman who was a top hit man for the mob. I would love to play him. Actually, it's sort of in the works, so I hope it goes through.

Channing Tatum

In my Olympic history I don't think I have achieved my potential as an athlete. That's what I want when I look back at my career. I want to be able to say I gave it my best shot.

Paula Radcliffe

It takes stamina to get up like an athlete every single night, seven to eight performances a week, 20 weeks in a row. And there are many young performers who only learn their craft in the two minute bits it takes to film a scene. You never learn the arc of storytelling, the arc of a character that way.

Kevin Spacey

I have been a Cowboys fan since I was a little bitty boy. And my dream has finally become a reality, of not only just playing a professional, becoming a professional athlete, but playing for the team that I always wanted to play for.

Emmitt Smith

When I started out as a little kid, I didn't say 'I just want to run football.' I wanted to be a great athlete.

Herschel Walker

When I was a kid, I was always an athlete. I played a lot of sports. I played football, basketball, baseball and soccer.

Scott Caan

You need to become more than one type of athlete. You have to be a sprinter, a weight man and a distance guy all in one.

Dan O'Brien

I've seen myself do stuff on stage that was pretty amazing. I think that would be true for any athlete. Any top athlete will see something that they are very proud of. All my injuries will attest to the fact that besides being a musician, it comes down to being an athlete.

Paul Stanley

We always spend more time on the throwing events and a little bit more on the long jump. They're my weaker events - they don't come as naturally to me as running and jumping. I like the hurdles and the high-jump, I'm a springy, speedy athlete so those suit me.

Jessica Ennis

I have to play baseball to make me happy. I have to be an athlete. But when it's all said and done, I'll be a normal father. A normal-type house man.

Rickey Henderson

Ruth was probably the greatest athlete to perform in any sport. Never has there been anybody like him.

George Steinbrenner

If we carry on filling up the calendar, we keep on pushing the athlete, we shorten the athletes longevity. The risk is to shorten a career that could have lasted 10 years because the athlete is burnt out.

Alberto Juantorena

In my neighborhood in Springfield, Ohio, there were a lot of young kids. We all played tackle football after school, but I knew very early on that I was not an athlete.

John Legend

I want to prove to people who sit on a couch and don't do anything but criticize other people that, if you're a true athlete or martial artist, you're not old until you can't get up and walk around anymore.

Herschel Walker

Unlike the traditional athlete, I've got to do more than just engage in my sport to put food on the table. When I'm done running, it's straight to the office.

Dean Karnazes

My dad was a good athlete. My mom had longevity. There were some athletic genes that certainly got passed down.

Hale Irwin

Not winning a title gives fuel to sportswriters and talking heads who question an athlete's true value.

Don Yaeger

I think cricket is there in Usain Bolt's blood. Since I got to watch from close quarters, it was amazing to see him run up to bowl. The perfect delivery stride is understandable because he is a world champion athlete. But the manner - he loaded at the crease and then bowled the ball - left me zapped. He looked like a natural cricketer.

Harbhajan Singh

If you can miss getting up in the morning and running into a wall, I miss playing football. I'll never be a frustrated athlete.

Brian Bosworth

Let's not call physical comedy falling down and pratfalls. All humor is physical, no matter how you dish it out. It's timing, like a dancer or an athlete would have.

Chevy Chase

On days when I do not work, I am working on my image. I have to hit the gym. I have beauty appointments. I have to work toward my next job and maintaining my image, just like an athlete.

Linda Evangelista

I'm an athlete, so I can get up one day and run and it wouldn't bother me. I don't get the time because I work for long hours every day. Being constantly on the move itself helps me stay fit. I don't go to a gym. I use the stairs, not the lift. I'm not into fitness, but I feel I should start ,as it's healthy.

Genelia D'Souza

But I like to think an athlete is an athlete.

Oscar Robertson

I always wanted to be a professional athlete, it just took me a while to realise it would be in racing. I played field hockey competitively for Ontario since I was 13, 14. Then I tried for the national side and made it. But it was so competitive. The girls were just so big and strong. I was getting crushed.

Chantal Sutherland

Each great athlete must some day bow to that perennial old champion, Father Time, even as I, for Time eventually wins.

Major Taylor

I've never felt that I was less of an athlete or not accomplished athletically because I didn't win an Olympic medal. It's definitely something I would have liked to have added to my resume, but at the same time I think I can look back at my athletic career and feel that I was one of the best.

Mary Decker

You can't control what the other athlete is going to do; you can't control anything except for your competition and how you execute the race or how you execute the task.

Michael Johnson

I didn't want to be a dancer. I just did it to work my way through college. But I was always an athlete and gymnast, so it came naturally.

Gene Kelly

The biggest thing for me with charity is awareness. Obviously as an athlete, I have an opportunity to make people more aware. The average person doesn't have that opportunity, so the best way is to spare some money, clothing, food - something. Most of us have a little excess of something that we can give.

Landon Donovan

Both parents supported my becoming a world class athlete.

Edwin Moses

My first year of college was tough. I thought that just being an athlete I could get by. I thought I was okay until I got kicked out, which happened twice.

Victor Cruz

My father's encouragement is what has brought me this far, because when I grew up I wanted to be like him, and I knew I had that ability to become an athlete. Being an Olympian is one of the greatest things, and being an Olympic gold medallist is one of the most prestigious titles in the world.

David Rudisha

In every school, more boys wanted to be remembered as a star athlete than as a brilliant student.

James S. Coleman

As a competitor and an athlete, you love that you get to go back and challenge someone, especially the world champs.

Tony Romo

I'm a jock and I'm an athlete, and that's what I love to do.

Marion Jones

With the responsibility of being a professional athlete, I believe that it is on us to go out there and help people.

Torrey Smith

I respect Georges St. Pierre as a businessman and an athlete. I don't have anything against him personally. But he's not the kind of fighter I like watching.

Ronda Rousey

www.ingramcontent.com/pod-product-compliance
Lightning Source LLC
Chambersburg PA
CBHW071217280526
45787CB00002B/707